CW00742555

Eyes wide open
Issues of economics, environment, wealth creation and distribution

Steve Bradbury with Allan Harkness

The Changemakers! series is published by Scripture Union and TEAR Australia

Eyes wide open: issues of economics, environment, wealth creation and distribution.
© Scripture Union Australia, 2000

Scripture Union books are published in Australia by
Scripture Union Australia
Resources for Ministry Unit
PO Box 77
Lidcombe
NSW 1825, Australia

Unless otherwise stated, Scriptures quoted are from the *New Revised Standard Version* Bible, © 1989, Division of Christian Education of the National Council of the Churches of Christ in the United States of America. Used by permission.

National Library of Australia Cataloguing-in-Publication Data

Bradbury, Steve.
Eyes wide open: issues of economics, environment, wealth creation and distribution.

ISBN 0 949720 88 7

Wealth - Religious aspects. I. Harkness, Allan. II. Scripture Union Australia. III. TEAR Australia. IV. Title. V. Title: Issues of economics, environment, wealth creation and distribution. (Series: Changemakers!)

241.68

All rights reserved. No portion of this publication may be reproduced by any means without the written permission of the publisher.

Cover Design and typesetting by
Openbook Publishers, Adelaide, SA.
Cover photo © TEAR Australia

CONTENTS

INTRODUCTION

It was at the turbulent age of 14 going on 15 when I made the radical decision to follow Christ, much to the surprise and occasional consternation of my parents.

With this about-turn it was not surprising that I decided to join the large and energetic Scripture Union that made waves in my high school.

Important friendships developed with Christian teachers and peers, and I discovered the richness that ought to characterise Christian fellowship.

It was in this context that I learned of the immense importance of the Bible.

No sooner had I come to faith than I was taught, and believed, that this special book was a manual from God – given to show us how we must live.

That conviction remains with me today, and it explains why I have sweated over this small series of studies.

There are times when it seems to me that nearly every page of the Scriptures contains evidence of God's abiding love for the poor, his deep mercy, and his passion for justice.

My great hope is that this series will encourage many Christians to examine this evidence, and in so doing allow the Holy Spirit to dig deeply into their hearts and minds.

If this were to happen, I couldn't even begin to predict the consequences.

Steve Bradbury
National Director, TEAR Australia

Photo: © Mike Webb Tearfund (UK)

To reflect on

To reflect on

Study One: 'If I were a rich man...'

Study One:

'Wealth in the scriptures is a grave spiritual danger. It blinds one's eyes to the values of the Kingdom, it twists priorities, and is the major distraction to the true service of God. It chokes the seed of the word, and blinds one to the needs of the poor.'
Chris Sugden

'IF I WERE A RICH MAN...'

Preparation for this session

Provide a felt-tip pen and sheet of A3 size paper (or slightly larger) for each participant.

minutes 5-10

Introduction

Have you ever participated in a vigorous Bible study about money and materialism or your standard of living?

(It's certainly not a topic that wins the popularity stakes in most church Bible study groups!)

• **What is it about the subject of money that we find so threatening?**

• **Quickly go around the group members and encourage one another to suggest a possible reason.**

Because the topic of money can generate stress and anxiety, pray before you proceed.

Invite the Holy Spirit to give you the ability to be honest with yourselves and each other as you read from the Bible and discuss together. Ask for both understanding and gentleness.

NB: The greater the level of openness within the group, the greater the impact this study is likely to have.

10-15 minutes

What is wealth?

Give each person a felt-tip pen and sheet of paper (A3 or larger).

Have each person complete this sentence, *'A person is economically wealthy when ...'*, then write this down in letters large enough for others to read.

• **Compare sentences. What are the points of consensus?**

• **Areas of divergence?**

In the light of your answers, try to decide on a common definition of what it means to be 'economically wealthy'.

On the basis of the group's findings, how wealthy do members consider themselves to be?

Use the line below to help answer this:

0	1	2	3	4	5	6	7	8	9	10

Absolutely   Moderately   Fantastically
Un-wealthy   wealthy   wealthy

Identify what it is about wealth that makes it so attractive to pursue.

25-35 minutes

Rich advice

Read 1 Timothy 6:17-19.

The following questions will help you understand the passage.

I were a rich man...' Photo: © Matt Wade TEAR Australia

1. What three pieces of strong advice does Paul tell Timothy to pass on to rich Christians?

2. Identify the different sorts of wealth contrasted in these verses.

• **What results from the accumulation of these sorts of wealth?**

3. What types of arrogance (v.17 = being 'haughty' or proud) do you associate with rich people?

• **Why is this an 'occupational hazard' for them?**

• **Suggest reasons why Paul felt the need to highlight this problem specifically.**

4. Picture someone 'set(ing) their hopes on the uncertainty of riches' (v.17).

• **What images come to mind?**

• **What difference, if any, is there between what Paul is discouraging here and a Christian** buying into, say, a generous superannuation package or setting aside substantial savings for a 'rainy day' or retirement?

5. Paul identifies a different sort of wealth in v.18 – 'rich in good works'.

• **What does this 'richness' reflect of the character of God?**

• **What is the 'life that really is life' in v.19?**

• **What is the connection between this and acquiring riches?**

6. Compare the wealth of vv.18-19 with your own definitions of economic wealth in the section, 'What is wealth', above.

• **What impact might building up wealth of either of these types have on our capacity to build up the 'treasure' of v.19?**

7. Think of any teaching or parables of Jesus that relate to, or contradict Paul's teaching in this passage.

8. If you have time, how would you respond to the following statement made by a fellow Christian?

'Just because you have wealth doesn't necessarily mean you love money. Christians can develop a healthy attitude to money, walk in the blessing and prosperity of God, and never have a problem with money again.'

minutes 10-20

'Enough is enough'

In the 1970's, John V. Taylor wrote a classic work on wealth and lifestyle. It was called *Enough is enough,* that is, living at an level appropriate for a Christian, rather than assuming that as a Christian you should live at the level appropriate for (or above!) your income.

- **But, what is 'enough'?**

1. What is enough for you in your particular situation?

- **List the steps or processes you might go through to work this out.**

2. How can we help one another in these processes?

- **What are the barriers to helping one another?**

3. Brainstorm together about what you and fellow-Christians could do with what is 'left over' if you lived at a level of 'enough'.

4. Think beyond your own horizons.

- **What ideas are sparked off by this quote?**

'In a world of limited resources our wealth is at the expense of the poor.

To put it simply, if we have it, others cannot.'

Richard Foster

5. If the group feels comfortable about discussing the topic, talk with one another about whether or not you found conversation threatening in this session.

5-10 *minutes*

Reflection and prayer

Read the following:

'Wealth in the scriptures is a grave spiritual danger.

It blinds one's eyes to the values of the Kingdom, it twists priorities, and is the major distraction to the true service of God.

It chokes the seed of the word, and blinds one to the needs of the poor.'

Chris Sugden

1. Without discussion, move into a time of silent personal reflection on the relevance and urgency of the matters raised by this study.

2. Pray as a group. Use the time as an opportunity before God to reflect further on the insights gained. 'Conversational prayer' may be especially appropriate here.

See *Praying Together* (Allan Harkness, Scripture Union & JBCE, p. 3).

Until your next meeting

Make a conscious effort to keep track of your spending for 1-2 weeks.

- **Evaluate the extent to which you are living within or beyond 'enough', as determined by the group.**

- **As you do this, pay careful attention to your attitudes.**

- **As opportunity arises, speak with other Christians about their understanding of the place of wealth in their lives.**

- **Question them about how they decided on an appropriate standard of living.**

Preparation for the next session

Ask a group member to prepare the Bible reading (Luke 12:13-21) for a dramatic retelling of the story, concentrating on how emphasis, phrasing and expression can be used for effect.

Have on hand a large sheet of newsprint and several felt-tip pens.

Notes:

Photo: Paul Mercer © TEAR Australia

To reflect on

Study Two: Greed kills

'One's life does not consist in the abundance of possessions.'
Luke 12:15

GREED KILLS

minutes **8-10**

Introduction

Update from the first session

Encourage group members to share insights gained since the first session.

Use the experiences and perspectives shared as a basis of prayer for each other. Invite God's Spirit to 'teach, rebuke, correct and train for right living' (2 Timothy 3:17), through this time together.

This session

Money has a way of making itself a preoccupation for us. If we consider ourselves poor, despite the clear warnings of the Bible, we are likely to 'want to be rich' (1 Timothy 6:9).

If we are wealthy, we are likely to some extent to have fallen into the trap of setting 'our hopes on the uncertainty of riches' (1 Timothy 6:17).

A frequent companion of money is greed. Together they can effectively distract us from loving God and loving our neighbours.

Jesus had much to say on the subject, which is not surprising. Initially, his radical perspective baffled and worried his disciples (Mark 10:23-27).

In this study we will be spectators of an incident in which an unusual request was made regarding money and possessions. Jesus tells a story to challenge his hearers to get their priorities right. This story presents a similar challenge for many Christians today.

minutes for whole section

30-45

Rich fools, arise!

Ask a group member to read Luke 12:13-21 as if they were telling the story, adding dramatic effects with appropriate emphasis and expression.

As the passage is read, members should note any emotions aroused in them by the story.

10-15 *minutes*

Take care! (vv.13-15)

1. Encourage members to describe their initial response to the story without discussing contributions.

2. Jesus' response to the request of the man in the crowd seems quite sharp.

- **Why do you think this was?**
- **What might the man's request indicate about relationships within his own family?**

3. Disputes over inheritance can often create grievances within families – or aggravate old ones.

- **Why does this happen?**
- **Group members who have had such experiences may like to share briefly how these affect family relationships.**

4. 'One's life does not consist in the abundance of possessions.' (v.15).

- **Expand on what you think Jesus meant when he said this.**

5. Greed can take a variety of forms.

- **How many of these can your group identify?**
- **From your knowledge of Jesus' teaching, why did he give such an urgent warning about greed?**

minutes  15-20

'You fool...!' (vv.16-21)

1. What does this parable suggest is the reason this foolish man acquired his wealth?

- **Is this similar to explanations people around** you give for their wealth (or for not being poor)?

2. The rich man had a 'fatal flaw'.

- **What was it?**

3. Make a list of the features which would help you differentiate between the rich man of this parable and someone who is 'rich toward(s) God' (v.21).

4. Divide into four sub-groups.

- **Have each group take one of the following passages: Deuteronomy 8:17-18; Psalm 95:3-5; Proverbs 12:27; and Amos 5:11-13.**
- **What special insight does your passage give concerning the creation of wealth?**
- **How might you use this idea in conversation**

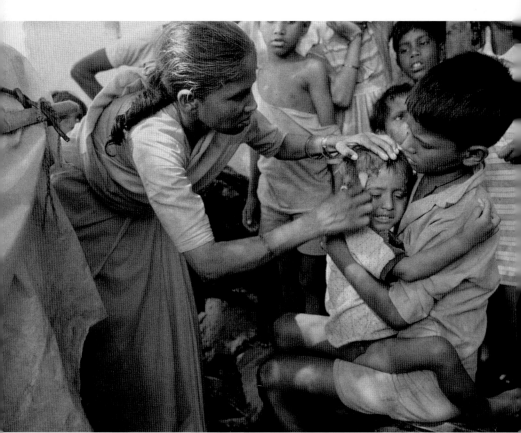

Photo: © TEAR Australia. Rich in good deeds.

with someone like the rich man of the parable?
• Share your discoveries with the full group.

5. If you have time, consider Zacchaeus (Luke 19) as another example of 'a rich fool'.

• What dynamics were at work in his life?

• What changes occurred as a result?

• Identify principles from Zacchaeus' experience for today's Christians.

Review

Ask the group to suggest a series of short statements summarising a Christian perspective on the accumulation of wealth.

Write these on a large sheet of paper. Some examples are:

• God is wonderfully generous towards us and wants us to be generous too in responding to the needs of others (1 John 3:16-18);

• The gains of our work are not just for ourselves but are meant to help support others in need (Ephesians 4:28);

• The raw materials necessary for the creation of wealth and our productive capacities are God-given;

•

Rich Christians in today's world

Read the following:

'Global Christianity is wealthy. Christians make up only one-third of the world's people, but we receive about two-thirds of the world's total income each year.

Tragically, we spend about 97% of this vast wealth on ourselves!

1% goes to secular charities. A mere 2% goes to all Christian work.

But even that tiny 2% we give to Christian causes is largely spent on ourselves, i.e. in our home congregations and in our home countries.'

Ronald Sider, *Evangelism and Social Action*, Hodder and Stoughton, London, 1993, p. 191.

2. Allow members to give an initial reaction to this comment.

3. How accurately does Sider's comment reflect your particular Christian community?

4. Identify what forces drive this state of affairs.

• Relate your discussion to your insights from the Bible passages above.

• What can be done to oppose these powerful forces, thus enabling Christians to share more generously?

5. From the range of ideas suggested, encourage either the whole group and/or each person to decide on one achievable action that they could take in the next month relating to their attitude towards wealth and its practical use.

- **If they wish, members can share their proposed action with the group.**

Reflection and prayer

Allow for a time of quiet to reflect on Jesus' perspective on creating and having wealth, as presented in this session.

Move into a time of unhurried prayer, perhaps as a whole group.

Allow time also for people to pray specifically for each other's commitment to action, in pairs or triplets.

Until the next session

Use the proposed action to guide your personal behaviour.

Use Jesus' perspective as a check on your attitude towards wealth and greed.

• **Note down your discoveries and reflections in a diary or journal.**

Preparation for the next session

Request a member to prepare Luke 16:19-31 as a dramatic story, with Jesus as the storyteller.

Notes:

Photo: © Matt Wade/TEAR Australia

To reflect on

To reflect on

Study Three: Scraps for the poor

Study Three:

'There is great suffering and poverty in the global "village". Can you imagine trying to survive on the equivalent of US$1 per day (about the cost of half a hamburger) or less? In some countries, more than half of the population is in this situation.'
Steve Bradbury

SCRAPS FOR THE POOR

minutes 10

Introduction

Update from the first session

Take a few minutes to review the topic of Session 2 and to hear from each other any significant experiences and insights that have occurred since then.

Take time to commit each other and this session to God.

Invite God's Spirit to challenge you to 'allow the Bible which we read to become the book which reads us!'

This session

Unless we have lived in a Third World country or in the poorest districts of some large western cities, we may never have been directly confronted by extreme poverty.

This could tempt us to gloss over the significance of Jesus' story about Lazarus and the rich man, which would be a sad mistake.

The story places all wealthy Christians under the spotlight, regardless of geographic location.

It also compels us to consider a core principle of discipleship that has eternal implications.

15-25 minutes

A shocking story

Imagine the group is part of a crowd listening to Jesus.

Divide your 'crowd' into two: one half is poor (the beggar-class) and the other half rich (maybe not as rich as the story's 'villain', but relatively rich nevertheless). Rearrange the seating, placing members of each group together.

Ask someone to read Luke 16:19-31 as if they were Jesus.

Separate into the two groups of the poor and the rich. Playing your *role*, decide your likely reaction to Jesus' story.

[Keep within your roles – at this stage you are not being asked for your personal opinions.]

Note that in the Palestine of Jesus' day, the opening scene (vv.19-21) would not have appeared unusual to either group.]

Come together again as a whole group or into sub-groups with a mixture of 'poor' and 'rich'. Have each group summarise their reactions or thoughts to 'the other group'.

[Again, remember to stay *in role*. Feel free to debate with one another.]

Move out of your roles.

Allow adequate time for the whole group to debrief on the dynamics of what happened between the two groups when role-playing.

From this, identify key insights about the significance of this story in Jesus' teaching.

The global Lazarus

We live in a global 'village' and throughout the village there is great suffering and poverty.

Imagine trying to survive on the equivalent of US$1 per day or less (about the cost of half a hamburger). In some countries, more than half of the population is in this situation.

Even at the best of times, people with this kind of income struggle to make ends meet. When crises arise, millions are plunged into Lazarus-like conditions.

Recently there have been many examples of this in different regions, such as,

Illness, crop failure, the loss of a job (even when normal wages are grossly and unjustly inadequate, this is a significant loss).

These are just a few of the factors that force *individuals and families* into dependence upon the casual charity of others.

Flood, drought, cyclones, and war. These can propel entire communities into famine or refugee queues.

1. Share as honestly as possible the extent to which you are affected by some current crises you have read about, seen or heard of, where people are suffering.

2. If someone in your group has personal experience of intense poverty, invite them to talk about it.

Photo: © Tearfund (UK)

3. Reflect on the extent to which rich people can have real understanding of the circumstances and pressures faced by the Lazaruses of this world.

Careless disregard

1. In the Bible passage you read, note that Abraham offers no reason for the rich man's punishment.

• **What does this suggest?**

2. In v.28, a warning is implied, which Jesus' hearers would identify and appreciate.

• **What is the likely content of the warning?**

3. What teaching from 'Moses and the prophets' (v.29) would be relevant for rich people to consider?

• **Some examples are Exodus 22: 25-27; 23:10-11; Deuteronomy 15:7-11; Isaiah 58:6-7; Jeremiah 5:23-29.**

4. Summarise what this story tells us about the heart-felt concerns of the only One who has risen from the dead?

[Note the content of the chapters immediately surrounding this story in Luke's Gospel.]

• **Express the thoughts of the group in one or two brief sentences.**

Reflection and prayer

Read the following:

'When money remains as private accumulation, not being shared, it stands over against Jesus Christ who has identified with the hungry, the naked, the homeless, the sick and those persecuted for the sake of justice.

As an end in itself it becomes an instrument of Satan (Acts 5:3), to exploit (Luke 19:8, James 5:1-6) and cause misery (Luke 16:19ff) to others.'

Andrew Kirk

In the light of this comment and the study of the Bible passage above, reflect upon the following questions:

1. From the poor identified in the section above, 'The Global Lazarus', who could be considered to be most needful of my/our attention?

2. What can I/we do to see the poor increasingly from Jesus' perspective?

3. How can I/we demonstrate care for the poor in a way that reflects Jesus' heartbeat for them?

4. What particular challenge comes to me/us for the coming weeks?

• **Allow unhurried time for both individual and group prayer.**

• **Pray specifically for yourself and for the poor who you have already started to see with the eyes of Jesus, simply by identifying them as needy.**

[An appropriate group method of prayer known as 'Incarnational praying' can be found in *Praying Together*, pp. 18f.]

Until the next session

- **Take time to delve further into 'Moses and the Prophets' to discover insights relevant to the story of the rich man and Lazarus.**

  For example, scan through Exodus chs. 21—23, Leviticus ch. 19, and/or any of the prophets (Isaiah – Malachi).

- **Re-examine your spending and saving in the light of God's heart for the poor.**

  Think both as individuals, and as members of the Christian community in which you are active.

- **Determine one situation to which you could help make a difference.**

- **Then take the appropriate practical steps towards this.**

Preparation for the next session

Bring:

Felt-tip pens and 10-12 strips of newsprint or computer paper of approximately 60cm x 20cm.

A large sheet of newsprint.

Notes:

Photo: © Phil Wilkerson

Conclude by saying this prayer together:

Generous God, through the poverty of Christ we have all become wealthy. Soften our hearts until we all freely share the good things we possess. May the rich obtain liberty and the poor their inheritance.

Bruce D. Prewer, *Brief Prayers for Australians*, Lutheran Publishing House, Adelaide, 1991, p. 37.

Photos: © Mike Webb Tearfund (UK) and Matt Wade TEAR Australia

To reflect on

Study Four: Whose earth?

'The earth has enough for every man's need,
but not for every man's greed.'
Mahatma Gandhi

WHOSE EARTH

minutes 10

Introduction

Take time for an update

Encourage group members to report on their discoveries and actions since the previous session.

Try to perceive where God has been at work in your lives and in the lives of others for whom you have been praying.

Commit this session to God – especially that you recognise God as the creator and sustainer of all things.

Introduction to this session

Imagine standing in a supermarket aisle. It's decision time...

Will I buy the environment-friendly, biodegradable soap or the efficient detergent which will quickly make my dishes squeaky-clean?

Will I buy the pretty pink-with-flowers and soft-on-the-bottom toilet paper or the khaki coloured stuff made from re-cycled, non-bleached paper?

Questions of this kind trouble the minds of environment-sensitive consumers. There are other, more complex questions as well...

- **How acceptable is my level of energy consumption – electricity, gas, petrol, etc.?**
- **Which banking institution has the best record of ethical decision-making for my superannuation investments?**
- **... and so on.**

What relevance do these questions have to Christian faith? And how and where do they intersect with the problems of global poverty?

This session examines issues of stewardship and care, issues that are vital to the health of our planet and to the well-being of God's creation.

Usually, our attitude to this topic is closely aligned with our attitudes towards injustice and poverty.

5-10 minutes

Every second counts

Ask a group member to read aloud the poem, 'Every second counts'.

Every second,
Another acre of forest
Is shaved
From the world's receding hairline.
Every hour we pump more poison
Under the earth's fragile skin,
Each deposit
Its own toxic land mine.
Every day
An irreplaceable
Whale-voice-choir
Performs
Its final song. ✝
Every week another crowd,
Beyond counting,
Joins a queue for bread
A billion bellies long.
Every month
The world's deserts
Eat more fertile land,
Like rust on a Skoda,
Only faster. ✳
Every year millions die
Through planet mis-management

Still mis-named
Natural Disaster.
Every morning
As we read
The Earth's vital signs,
The signs of death
Become clearer and clearer: ✳
And every time
We close our eyes
And turn from the truth,
We bring that death
Several steps
Nearer.

Gerard Kelly

From a Tearfund UK publication, *3rd Track,* Issue 11, April 1992. Reproduced by permission.

- **Discuss your reactions to this poem.**

Photo: © Jonathon Young Tearfund (UK). Tree planting in Nepal.

- **The following questions may help you do this, but don't let them restrict your discussion.**

1. The poem describes an impending crisis.

- **How real in fact is this crisis?**

2. Describe the link between the destruction of forests and hungry bellies.

3. Gerard Kelly thinks 'planet mis-management' is a more appropriate term than 'natural disaster'.

- **What are the likely reasons for his thinking this?**

4. Brainstorm together for contemporary examples of planet mis-management.

- **Rank these according to how serious you consider the mis-management to be. [Note what criteria you use to determine the level of 'seriousness'.]**

10-20 minutes

Using or abusing God's creation?

The Bible can help us identify important principles for how to shape the way we use Earth's resources.

- **Divide into pairs and allocate these passages:**

Genesis 1:1-31; Leviticus 25:23-24; Psalm 19:1-6; Psalm 24:1-2; Psalm 104: 5-30; Psalm 115:16; Matthew 6:26,28; Luke 12:13-21; Acts 4:32-35; Romans 8:19-23.

- **In pairs, clarify the environment-related principle contained in your passage(s).**

- **Write the principle on a strip of paper. Report back to the full group.**

- **Add other biblical principles not raised in these passages which you think are important that concern the use of the world's resources.**

- In the light of these principles, try to determine what could be a 'responsible level of consumption' for people in your situation.

The link between the environment and poverty

Read these two comments:

'The earth has enough for every man's need, but not for every man's greed.'
Mahatma Gandhi

'The effect of the Fall was that the desire for growth became obsessive and idolatrous, the scale of the growth became excessive for some at the expense of others, and the means of growth became filled with greed, exploitation and injustice.'
Christopher Wright

- To what extent do these two quotes synchronise with the biblical principles on the root causes of the abuse and misuse of the earth's resources on one hand, and massive global poverty on the other?
- What passages of Scripture can you identify which would support the comments of these two people?
- Are there any passages you can point to which would support an opposing point of view?
- If so, how would you summarise the environmental implications of these passages?

A practical exercise

Step One. Divide a large sheet of paper into three columns:

Column A.
What individuals can do to reduce consumption of the earth's resources to a responsible level.

Column B.
How many people in your group are attempting these practices

Column C.
How often in the past 2 years this area has been commented on in some aspect of your church life

Step Two. List in the first column as many distinct items as members suggest, then complete columns 2 and 3.

1. Look at the finished chart.

- **What does this exercise indicate?**

2. Few Christian groups or congregations make much effort to address important environmental concerns.

- **Why are the reasons for this?**
- **What could your group do to get such concerns onto the agenda of your church?**

3. Reducing our consumption levels is a very practical contribution we can make to good earth-management practice, but often we are hindered by broader national and international agendas.

- **Discuss the range of difficulties you encounter as you try to follow biblical principles in your management of resources.**

4. From the list of ideas created in the left-hand column of the chart, select items in which members are personally interested.

• With one or two like-minded members of the group, talk about specific steps that could be taken to bring about change in each area.

minutes 10

Reflection and prayer

Preparation for prayer

Briefly recall the key ideas and concerns that have been raised through this session. Remember the significance of the direct connection between poverty and the environment.

Recognise also the extent to which the Christian understanding of human nature bears on this connection:

'Destroying the environment is a major cause of world famine. Since God calls us to be concerned about the poor and to feed the hungry, we must save the environment for the sake of the poor and for the sake of the hungry.'

Tony Campolo

Pray for four areas of concern

1. For greater awareness of God's deep concern for creation and of your own impact upon the environment.

Consider including elements of praise and thanksgiving (*'God saw everything that he had made, and indeed, it was very good'* – Genesis 1), as well as confession.

2. For those who are forced to eke out a living on already damaged and marginal land and those who live in poverty because of the environmental decisions made at national and international levels.

3. For yourself and your church. Ask the Holy Spirit to show how you might become more faithful nurturers and managers of God's creation.

Ask too how you might be able to link a more just consumption pattern with a more faithful response to the needs of the poor, at both an individual and church level.

4. For the will and determination, despite distractions, to take the practical steps in the section, 'A Practical Exercise' above.

Until the next session

• **Make an agreement with at least one other member of your group to be accountable for the specific action you have decided upon.**

Plan to make contact at least weekly (by telephone, email, or in person), for mutual support, encouragement and prayer.

• **Pay careful attention to any environmental issues raised – in your community, nationally or internationally.**

Keep a log of what you observe.

Preparation for the next session

Poster-sized paper and several felt-tip pens

Songs or hymns on the topics of the Lordship of Jesus Christ over the nations and the role of Christians in seeking to bring about change.

Paper/envelopes for people to write a letter.

Notes:

Photo: © Mike Webb Tearfund (UK)

To reflect on

To reflect on

Study Five: The politics of poverty

Study Five:

"Rescue the weak and needy."
Psalm 82:4a

THE POLITICS OF POVERTY

minutes **10**

Introduction

Update since the previous session

Allow time for members to report on their experiences and observations since the previous session.

Identify areas in which you need special encouragement or help. Use the feelings expressed and insights shared as a natural opportunity for prayer.

Introduction to this session

Politics is a subject best avoided in Christian small groups if we want to keep our fellowship intact!

Discussions on political issues tend to raise the room temperature and polarise people. Rather than risk this, we often treat politics as a taboo subject and restrict agendas to 'matters of faith'.

This creates a danger for we quickly develop an understanding of the Christian faith and a practice of religion condemned by the Bible itself.

If we keep our religion privatised, it doesn't need to address situations and injustices that grieve and anger God.

It can even encourage us to count as divine blessings those benefits we directly or indirectly receive from those same injustices.

The Bible is not a polite book! It does not avoid politics. Frequently we read of God's chosen spokespersons publicly challenging political leaders and their policies, a particularly risky business.

This probably explains why these people were often reluctant to take on the prophetic responsibility given to them by God.

When government works primarily for the interests of the rich and powerful, the exploitation of the weak and poor becomes the order of the day.

This study 'profiles' such governments and what God thinks of them.

We will explore the quality of government that God required from the rulers of Israel, a quality God still requires from the rulers of nations.

5 *minutes*

To start your thinking...

On a sheet of poster-sized paper make a list of the responsibilities your group members believe any government should take in relation to the people under its rule.

Don't enter into discussion at this stage, as you will refer to the list later in this session.

Government as predator

Read Ezekiel 22:23-31. [Historical note: Here the leaders of the nation of Israel are addressed by Ezekiel (most likely sometime in the 6th century BC), who is pointing out how the fall of Jerusalem and the collapse of the nation is now inevitable.]

1. What is specifically described in this passage?

2. Select from the following list words that best describe the exploitation described in this passage:

Random, comprehensive, structural, opportunistic, individualistic, and systematic.

Add your own words:

3. Who are the exploiters? In terms of motivation, status and opportunity, what do they have in common,?

What is it about their status or authority that enables them to succeed in their oppressive practices? (see also Ecclesiastes 5.8)

4. What do the victims have in common besides their suffering?

5. Look closely at Ezekiel's descriptions of the actions of the princes, priests, officials and prophets.

What does the language chosen by God and spoken through Ezekiel (v.23) reveal of God's attitudes?

Government as protector

Read Jeremiah 22:1-3, 13-17. [Historical note: Jeremiah was God's spokesperson to the southern nation of Judah in the 7th century BC.]

1. What practices was God totally opposing?

2. What were the essential actions or practices that God required of the King of Judah? What difference would such practices make for those members of society who were politically and economically weak?

3. Note the severity of God's promised punishments (Jeremiah 22:4-12, 18-23; Ezekiel 22:30-31). What does this reveal about the character of God?

Government as provider

Read Psalm 82.

[Note: The 'gods' (v.1) refer either to the 'gods' in whose name the surrounding kings claimed to rule, or to the kings themselves, who commonly claimed to be divine. The scene in the psalm describes a gathering of all the rulers on the earth.]

1. Suggest the primary concern of the psalm.

2. In Hebrew poetry, 'rhyming ideas' are common, with one idea often presented in a number of slightly different ways.

Identify the key focus of verses 3-4, then comment on the four overlapping but distinct responsibilities that God expects rulers to fulfil.

3. What are some of the ways by which rulers and judges 'defend the unjust' and 'show partiality to the wicked' (v.2)? (It may help to refer to previous passages you have looked at from Ezekiel and Jeremiah.)

4. What does this passage have to say to those who argue that 'we should not mix religion and politics'?

minutes 15-25

Meanwhile, in today's world ...

1. Think of some contemporary examples where governments could be accused of similar actions to those discussed in the three areas above. In which of the three areas could your national government be considered guilty, either recently or in your nation's history?

- **Identify which of your examples show severe cases of governments failing to fulfil God's mandate for rulers.**

2. Return now to the list of government responsibilities you listed at the beginning of the study. Quickly review that list, adding any further areas that come to mind.

- **In the light of the biblical data you have discussed, write a letter alongside each item according to how important you think that responsibility is:**

'A' = vitally important,

'B' = important,

'C' = less important.

- **How does your own government measure up against your criteria? [Note: be balanced in**

Photo: © Steve Bradbury TEAR Australia '...maintain the right of the lowly and destitute.' Psalm 82:3b

your evaluation – both affirm and criticise where it is due.]

3. Suggest areas in which your government could be more 'biblical' in its responsibilities, and practical ways in which you could help it to do so.

minutes 10

Reflection and prayer

• **Take time to pray for your own government and for governments in nations where injustice and oppression of the poor continue.**

Pray also for people and groups seeking to address these issues.

• **Ask the Spirit of Christ to convict you of areas in which you could be a change-agent – as individuals, a small group, a church fellowship, and/or part of a larger community.**

Pray too for the willingness and ability to model God's values for just and right government.

Make this prayer the basis for your own:

'Lord, in these times when we are about to lose hope and our efforts seem futile, grant that we may perceive in our hearts and minds the image of your resurrection which remains our only source of courage and strength, so that we may continue to face the challenges, and struggle against hardship and oppression born of injustice.'

– by people from a slum area in the Philippines. Found in *Prayers Encircling the World*, London, SPCK, 1998, p. 220.

If appropriate for your group, prayerfully sing several songs or hymns which affirm the Lordship of Jesus Christ over the nations of the world, and the role of Christians in seeking to bring about change.

Consider action that you could take as a response to this study:

• Write to the leadership of a nation (and/or that nation's diplomatic representative in your country) where abuse of basic human rights continues.

Express your concern politely but firmly, and ask for a response.

• If you believe your own government could be doing more to fulfil its God-given responsibility to provide for the poor and weak, write a letter urging change.

It is important to cite specific cases where you think more should be done or where there are injustices that need to be overturned.

• Explore the possibility of establishing a 'twinning' relationship between your group (or church) and a group working for change in another country, for mutual support and encouragement.

Contact TEAR Australia or Tearfund (UK) for the names of such groups in a country or region in which you have an interest.

Review this series of studies

• Allow a few minutes to quietly reflect on the five sessions in this book. Then invite each member to speak briefly about what has been most significant, encouraging, challenging, and/or disturbing for him or her.

• Talk together about appropriate practical steps that could be taken as a result of the insights gained in this study.

- Encourage members to each write a letter to God, saying what specific action they intend to take over the coming few weeks.

[Note: If you plan to meet in 4-6 weeks, take time to review these letters. Alternatively, use the support partnership developed from Session 4 for ongoing accountability.]

- Take time to draw all these threads together in prayer.

- Conclude by singing or saying together the *Prayer of St Francis of Assisi:*

> *Lord, make me an instrument of*
> *your peace.*
> *Where there is hate, let me sow love;*
> *Where there is injury, Lord, let me sow*
> *A pardon deep as the flowing sea.*
>
> *Where there is doubt, let me*
> *sow faith;*
> *Where there's despair, let me*
> *sow hope;*
> *Where there is darkness, let me*
> *sow light;*
> *Where there is pain, let me sow joy.*
>
> *O loving Lord, may I not seek*
> *To be understood, but to understand,*
> *To be consoled, but to console,*
> *Or to be loved, but to love man.*
>
> *For it's in giving that we receive;*
> *It's in forgiving, that we're forgiven;*
> *And it's in dying that we are born*
> *To eternal life, to eternal life.*

Notes:

FURTHER READING

Introductory

Andrews, Dave
   Can You Hear the Heartbeat (Hodder and Stoughton, 1989)

Rand, Stephen
   Guinea Pig For Lunch (Hodder and Stoughton, 1998)

Sider, R.
   Rich Christians in an Age of Hunger (Hodder and Stoughton, 1997)

Stott, J.
   Issues Facing Christians Today, 2nd Edition (HarperCollins, 1990)

More Advanced

Grigg, V.
   Companion to the Poor (Albatross, 1984)

Haugen, Gary A.
   Good News About Injustice (IVP, 1999)

Hughes, Dewi
   God of the Poor (OM, 1998)

Wallis, Jim
   The Soul of Politics (Harper Collins, 1995)

Wright, C.J.H.
   Living As The People Of God (IVP, 1983)

A wide range of relevant educational resources, including videos, magazines, information packs, youth and children's materials are available from **TEAR Australia and Tearfund.**

Contact Details

TEAR Australia

P.O. Box 289
Hawthorn 3122
Australia

Phone: (03) 9819 1900 or Toll Free 1800 244 986 Fax: (03) 9818 3586
E-mail: tearaust@tear.org.au Web site: www.tear.org.au

Tearfund

100 Church Road
Teddington, Middlesex TW11 8QE
United Kingdom

Phone: 0845 355 8355 Fax: (0)181 943 3594
E-mail: enquiry@tearfund.dircon.co.uk Web site: www.tearfund.org